DEAR PRUDENCE

A Victorian Lady Advises on Intimate
and Delicate Matters, including Drink,
Lust and the Marital Embrace

DEAR PRUDENCE

Being the Correspondence
between *Prudence* and many
Troubled Inquirers, discovered
and collected by Gerard Macdonald

CENTURY PUBLISHING
LONDON

Copyright © Gerard Macdonald 1985

All rights reserved

First published in Great Britain 1985
by Century Publishing Co Ltd
Portland House. 12–13 Greek Street. London WIV 5LE

Set in Linotron Bodoni by Input Typesetting Ltd

Printed and bound in Great Britain
by Anchor Brendon Ltd. Tiptree. Essex

ISBN 0 7126 1073 1

CONTENTS

SOURCES

Prudence's advice is drawn from the following authentic Victorian sources, indicated in the text by appropriate superscript numbers:

1. G. Bainton. *The Wife as Lover and Friend*. London: Clarke. 1895.
2. Thomas Baird. *Some Foes of Modern Society*. Hamilton. 1889.
3. Dr E. Blackwell. *Counsel to Parents on the Moral Education of their Children*. London: Hirst Smyth [sic]. 1878.
4. Rev. R. Ashington Bullen. *Our Duty as Teachers*. London: Social Purity Alliance. 1886.
5. Henry Butter. *Marriage for the Million*. London: W. H. Guest. 1875.
6. Charles Carroll. *The Tempter of Eve*. St Louis: The Adamic Publishing Co.. 1902.
7. Mrs E. S. Chesser. *From Girlhood to Womanhood*. London: Cassell. 1913.
8. Sir Thomas Clouston. *Before I Wed, or Young Men and Marriage*. London: Cassell. 1913.
9. Major Seton Churchill. *Betting and Gambling*. London: Nisbet. 1894.
10. Major Seton Churchill. *Forbidden Fruit for Young Men*. London: Nisbet. 1887.
11. A. C. Dutt. *Health Notes for the Seaside*. Whitby: Horne & Co.. 1895.
12. Alfred S. Dyer. *Facts for Men on Moral Purity and Health*. London: Dyer Brothers. 1884.
13. Ellis Ethelmer. *Baby Buds*. Congleton: Buxton House. 1895.
14. Ellis Ethelmer. *The Human Flower*. Congleton: Elmy. 1895.

15. *Ethics for Youth*. London: White. 1828.
16. *The Ethics of Love*. Walsall: W. Henry Robinson at the Steam Printing Works. 1881.
17. Dr C. F. Goss. *Husband, Wife and Home*. Philadelphia: Vir. 1901.
18. G. Zabriskie Gray. *Husband and Wife*. Boston: Houghton Mifflin. 1885.
19. Thos E. Green. *The Man-traps of the City*. Chicago: Revell. 1884.
20. J. E. Hazelwood. *The Knight of Purity*. Leeds: Inchbold & Beck. 1884.
21. Walter Heape. *Preparation for Marriage*. London: Cassell. 1894.
22. *How to Choose a Husband*. London: Partridge & Co.. 1856.
23. *The Husband that Will Suit You, and How to Treat Him*. Calcutta: Lewis & Company. n.d.
24. *The Illustrated Manners Book, a Manual of Good Behaviour & Polite Accomplishments*. New York: Leland Clay. 1885.
25. Mrs A. M. Longshore-Potts. *Love, Courtship and Marriage*. London: Hill Siffken. n.d.
26. P. Mantegazza. *The Art of Taking a Wife*. London: Gay & Bird. 1894.
27. *Manners of Modern Society*. London: Cassell. Petter & Galpin. n.d.
28. *The Manners of the Aristocracy, by One of Themselves*. London: Ward Lock and Company. n.d.
29. F. B. Meyer. *Love, Courtship & Marriage*. London: S. W. Partridge. 1899.
30. Charles H. Parkhurst. *Talks to Young Men*. London: T. Fisher Unwin. 1897.
31. Charles H. Parkhurst. *Talks to Young Women*. London: T. Fisher Unwin. 1897.
32. Anna Ruppert. *Dermatology: a Book of Beauty*. London: Anna Ruppert. 1887.
33. Dr Mary Scharlieb. *What it Means to Marry*. London: Cassell. 1913.
34. *Schoolboy Morality: an Address to Mothers*. London: Social Purity Alliance. 1886.
35. Brevard D. Sinclair. *The Crowning Sin of the Age: the Perversion of Marriage*. London: Marshall Bros. 1893.
36. Dr Sylvanus Stall. *Parental Honesty*. London: Vir. 1901.

37. Dr Sylvanus Stall. *What a Man of Forty-five Ought to Know.* Philadelphia: Vir. 1901.

38. Dr Sylvanus Stall. *What a Young Man Ought to Know.* London: Vir. 1897.

39. Alice B. Stockham. *Karezza: the Ethics of Marriage.* Chicago: A. B. Stockham & Co.. 1896.

40. T. de Witt Talmage. *The Marriage Ring.* New York: Funk & Wagnalls. n.d.

41. Samuel Hough Terry. *Controlling Sex in Generation: the Physical Law Influencing Sex in the Embryo of Man and Brute, and Its Direction to Produce Male or Female Offspring at Will.* New York: Fowler & Wells. 1885.

42. Alfred Ernest Tracey. *The Negro Problem: its Solution.* Trinidad: Daily News. 1895.

43. R. T. Trall. *Sexual Physiology: a Scientific and Popular Exposition.* New York. 1901.

44. R. T. Trall. *The Illustrated Family Gymnasium.* New York: S. R. Wells. 1879.

45. Phoebe Wardell. *Marrying and the Married.* London: Horace Marshall & Son.

46. E. Westermarck. *The Future of Marriage.* London: Macmillan. 1906.

47. Mrs Mary Wood-Allen. *What a Young Woman Ought to Know.* Philadelphia: Vir. 1898.

48. A Woman. *The Secret Book containing Private Information and Instruction for Women and Young Girls with Invaluable Information and Mature Counsel concerning the Duties of Parents, the Vices of Children, and the Blight of Womanhood.* London: Social Purity Alliance. 1886.

1
ON SELECTING A WIFE

Dear Prudence
I have been courting a Young Lady for three years next
Quarter Day. Should we consider Marriage?
                                        Impetuous Lover

Dear Impetuous
Time, says Mrs Longshore-Potts, 'is not much to be
considered. Some court five years, some court ten'.²⁵
Certainly a Refined Girl will not want to rush, with Inde-
cent Haste, into the Early Marriage which you so clearly
contemplate.
                                        Prudence

Dear Prudence
I am seeking a Wife. What should she Measure?
Please state whether this is With, or Without,
Undergarment.
                                        Worried Brown Eyes

Dear Worried
According to Mr Samuel Hough Terry, the prospective
wife 'should Measure, *over a single light Undergarment,*
at least 36 inches Bust measure under the Arms, 26 inches
Waist measure, and 38 inches around the Hips'.⁴¹
    Checking on these Facts may, of course, be a Delicate
Matter; but the Undergarment will preserve at least some
of the Proprieties.
                                        Prudence

'a somewhat Simian appearance'

Dear Prudence

My Fiancée has a low, broad Forehead, giving her a somewhat Simian appearance. Is this a Disadvantage?
                                                    Aesthetic Sensibility

Dear Aesthetic

It very much depends on her nose. Mr Bainton writes that 'some prefer a low, broad Forehead and contend it is a Mark of Beauty . . . but the Height of the Forehead should equal the length of the Nose'.[1]

Find some Pretext for Comparing these Features.
                                                    Prudence

2
On Entering the State of Matrimony

Dear Prudence
I am curious to know Why we can have only One Wife. Is
this God's decision?

Puzzled Inquirer

Dear Puzzled
It is. According to Dr Stall, 'if God had intended otherwise.
He would have removed every Rib in Adam's body, and
created a Plurality of Wives for him'.[38]

As well as being morally inadmissible, this would be
physically impossible. No one can survive without ribs.

Prudence

'He would have removed
every Rib in Adam's body'

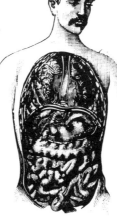

'It is the great mass of . . . Fetish Worshippers and Devil Worshippers who sanction Polygamy.'

Dear Prudence
What, then, of Polygamy?

Unsatisfied Inquirer

Dear Unsatisfied
I assumed you were considering Christians, not Fire Worshippers or Buddhists. 'Generally speaking, Monogamy is only adopted by Christian nations . . . It is the great mass of Hindus, Mohammedans, Buddhists, Fire Worshippers, Fetish Worshippers and Devil Worshippers who sanction Polygamy.'[10]

Prudence

Dear Prudence
My future Wife wishes to be married in the Afternoon. Is this Possible?

Potential Spouse

Dear Spouse
It entirely depends on whether you want to spend your Honeymoon in Australia; and for how long. The law is quite clear. 'The rite of marriage is to be performed between the hours of eight a.m. and twelve, upon pain of suspension and felony, with fourteen years' transportation.'[27]

Prudence

3
ON THE MARITAL EMBRACE

Dear Prudence
My Wife, who is Younger than I, desires a daily Marital
Embrace. Is this Unwise?
                                        A Weary Toiler

Dear Toiler
More than unwise, it is positively unhealthy. A well-known
doctor writes of Patients 'who for years indulged in Sexual
Intercourse as often as once in twenty-four hours, and
some who would have Indulged still oftener. Of course,
the Result was Premature Decay, and often Permanent
Invalidism'.[43]

I suggest you make your Insatiate Bride aware of this
– while you still can.
                                        Prudence

'. . . the Result was
Premature Decay'

Dear Prudence
I am ashamed to admit that
I have recently Experienced
a modicum of Enjoyment in
the Marital Embrace.
Doubtless this is not a
condition which should
continue?

Mrs E. de St J B ff

Dear Mrs E.
Indeed it should not: stop it
at once. Mr Terry writes
that 'when Intercourse is
confined to the sacred
privacy of the Marital
Chamber, the Mind should
Rise above the thought of
Personal Enjoyment, to the
Contemplation of the
Agencies that bring into
being an Immortal Soul'.[+1]

Prudence

'My wife has recently started to
Initiate the Marital Embrace'

Dear Prudence
My Wife has recently started to Initiate the Marital
Embrace. I have no doubt you will agree that this is
Improper as it is Unseemly.   *Mr E. de St J B ff*

Dear Sir
All Authorities agree that 'the Sexual Relationship must
be, not of the Woman seeking and Appropriating the
Man, but, of necessity, his Seeking and Appropriating
her'.[18] Further, 'there is no doubt about the fact that the
average Man is more Sexual than the average Woman,
and that when a Woman has borne Children her capacity
for Sexual Passion is still further decreased'.[21]
   The importunate Woman is, in short, an Offence against
Nature.   Prudence

Dear Prudence
My next-door Neighbours have Greasy Faces, and Tremble.
Is this the mark of Illness, or of Marital Excess?
                                  A Concerned Moralist

Dear Moralist
You are almost certainly seeing the evidence of Excess.
'Their lustreless Eyes, their sodden and greasy Faces, and
their trembling Hands, are evidences that an almost nightly
Indulgence is kept up of the pleasures of the Marriage
Bed.'[41]
                                  Prudence

4

ON THE DESIRABILITY OF PROCREATION

Dear Prudence
What agency determines the sex of the child as yet unborn?
An Anxious and Prospective Father

Dear Anxious
The testicle in which the Infant originates determines its
Sex. According to Dr D. F. Sixt, 'the right Testicle prod-
uces Male sperm cells . . . while the left Testicle produces
Female sperm cells.'[3]
Prudence

Dear Prudence
Concerning the left and right Testicle: can the Gender of
the Unborn Infant be made, in this way, a Matter of
Choice?
Prospective Begetter of Sons

Dear Begetter
You are in luck. 'It is only necessary that Right or Left
Testicle be firmly compressed, in the act of seminal
emission, to beget a Boy or a Girl.'[3]
It is fair to say, though, that Compressing the
appropriate Testicle, in the heat of the Marital Embrace,
is a physically demanding Exercise.
Prudence

Dear Prudence
I have followed the correspondence on Compression of the
Testicle with an Interest which borders on Anxiety. May

16

I ask help for those of us who are blessed with more than the Usual Number of Testicles?
A Worried and Multi-Testicled Person

Dear Multi-Testicles
I fear that Dr Sixt has little patience with you and your like. 'People of this kind,' he writes, 'are extremely scarce; and no rules can be laid down for Exceptions in cases where Nature herself has made an Exception to her own rules.'[43]

Prudence

Dear Prudence
I have aligned my Marriage Bed from North to South. Is this Orientation important at the moment of Conception?
Captain R von H

Dear Captain
It is; unless you actively desire to produce Deformed Hermaphrodites. An American writer has firmly stated that 'if the body of any animal be exactly on a line with the North and South Poles during the instant of Procreation, in ninety-nine cases out of every hundred conception will *not* take place; but if it should, the Offspring will be Deformed, and very probably a Hermaphrodite'.[43]

If I were you, I should move the Bed, before you do anything else.

Prudence

'unless you actively desire to produce Deformed Hermaphrodites'

17

*'a similar Appearance may
result from Dropsy'*

*Dear Prudence
I have observed that my
wife's Abdomen enlarges
by the Week; and that
she continually Salivates.
Could she, perhaps, be
Pregnant?
Uncertain Husband*

Dear Uncertain
According to Dr Trall, 'enlargement of the Abdomen is
apparent in Pregnancy, but a Similar Appearance may
result from Dropsy'[43]; you cannot, therefore, take the
matter as proven. Salivation, he adds, 'affects some women
during Pregnancy, but as a sign of Pregnancy it is to be
taken as an Exception, rather than the Rule'.

Have you thought, incidentally, of asking your Wife
whether she thinks she has Dropsy; or is in a Delicate
Condition?

Prudence

*Dear Prudence
It has now been Ascertained that my Wife is with Child.
She has stopped Salivating, but seems to become increas-
ingly Stupid. Could this be a part of Nature's Plan?*

Ever More Uncertain

Dear Ever More
Maternal stupidity is, indeed, a vital part of Nature's
Purpose. During pregnancy, 'the increased activity
demanded of some Organs tends to decrease the activity
of others. The Brain is the chief example of the latter
class'.[21]

Prudence

5

ON THE UNDESIRABILITY OF CHILDLESSNESS

Dear Prudence
My Wife and I are determined not to bring Offspring into the World. I take it that the Practice of Birth Control is now Morally Permissible?

       A Rationalist Spouse

Dear Rationalist
You could not be more mistaken. A childless couple, writes Mr Sinclair, 'are simply engaged in prostitution, without the infamy which attaches to that vice and crime'.[35] Birth control he describes as 'the cool and villainous contract by which people entering into the marital relation engage, in defiance of the laws of God and the laws of the Commonwealth, that they shall be unencumbered by a family of Children'.

       Prudence

Dear Prudence
In the Course of Daily Life I meet many Idiots. Are these the Outcome of attempted Birth Control? *Keen Observer*

Dear Observer
If you commonly frequent Asylums, then your Supposition is correct. The imbecile Asylums contain many Unfortunates whose Mental and Moral Natures are but the unerring fruition of parental effort to prevent their Being.[35]

 So much, dear Reader, for Contraception. Prudence

Dear Prudence

Since reading your Letter I have ceased the Practice of Birth Control. My Wife has now borne Twins who have reduced us to Destitution. Can this be a desirable Outcome?

A Destitute and Former Rationalist

Dear Destitute

According to Mr Sinclair, your present state is preferable to your former one. 'Let us remember that it is a thousandfold worse to Sin, and to pervert Marriage, and to Murder the Unborn by preventing Conception, than to raise a Family, even with the burden of Poverty and Debt.'[35]

No doubt you will find this some Comfort in your Straitened Condition.

Prudence

'The burden of Poverty and Debt'.

6

ON THE PROPER UPBRINGING
OF CHILDREN

Dear Prudence
My eldest Child, who is now of mature years, wishes to
take the occasional Cup of Tea. Should such Indulgence
be Permitted?
                                    Mother of Seven

Dear Mother of Seven
It should not, unless you wish to introduce among your
Innocent Brood a Debauchee and Sexual Dissipate. Tea,
according to one of our leading authorities, 'together with
Coffee and Flesh Meats – to say nothing of the abomin-
ations of the Baker and Confectioner – are sufficient to
account for the early tendency to Sexual Dissipation and
Debauchery manifested by a large portion of the Children
in our Primary Schools'.[43]
                                    Prudence

Dear Prudence
My first Female Infant, though walking well, speaks
indistinctly. How should I improve its Diction?
                                    Anxious Parent

Dear Anxious
'This habit may be readily corrected by reciting for ten or
fifteen minutes, two or three times a day, *with a gag*
placed vertically between the teeth. Commence with a gag
about half an inch in width, and once a week increase it a
quarter of an inch.'[44]
                                    Prudence

'My first Female Infant, though walking well, speaks indistinctly'

Dear Prudence
I hesitate to trouble you further, but exactly what should my Child recite with the Gag in her mouth?

Anxious Parent

Dear Anxious
Dr Trall suggests two introductory Exercises. First: 'On a sudden, open fly with impetuous recoil and jarring sound the infernal doors, and on their groaning hinges grate harsh thunder.' (To be recited harshly.) Second: 'As earth asleep unconscious lies; effuse your mildest beams, ye constellations, while your angels strike, amid the spangled sky, the silver lyre.' (To be recited harmoniously.)++

See what that does for your daughter's Diction.

Prudence

22

Dear Prudence
Poverty compels us to Accommodate both Sons and Daughters in a Single Room. Should we Invest in a second-hand Chair-Bedstead, to prevent Immorality?

An Impoverished Worker

Dear Impoverished
You are right in your instinct. The sooner you invest in the Chair-Bedstead, the Better.

According to Mr Dyer, 'a great deal of Immorality is caused by improper Sleeping Accommodation – the herding together of big boys and girls in one Bedroom'. But, he adds, 'expedients are not far to seek. A Chair-Bedstead, purchasable second-hand for a few shillings, and convertible in a few moments to an Easy Chair, can be made practically equivalent to another Bedroom.'[12]

Prudence

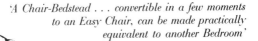

'A Chair-Bedstead . . . convertible in a few moments
to an Easy Chair, can be made practically
equivalent to another Bedroom'

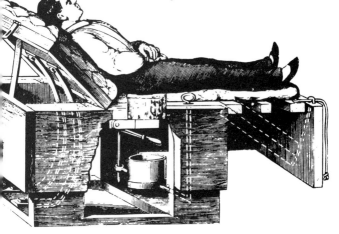

Dear Prudence
For speaking, Unchaperoned, with a Young Man of the
Opposite Sex, my Parents have Visited upon me Every
Sort of Punishment. Is this Just?
                                              Miss Angela C

Dear Angela C
Your parents are entirely correct. In the words of Mr
Mantegazza, 'if you throw yourself Head Foremost into
a Bottomless Abyss only to satisfy Carnal Excitement which
you may call Passion, but which is only Desire of the
Flesh – then Father and Mother have Full Right to oppose
your Ruin with *all possible Means*'.[26]

                                              Prudence

Dear Prudence
I am considering the occasional Walk with my Children,
pointing out to them the Poorer Classes and the Sons of
Toil. Would you recommend such an Exercise?
                                              Colonel J R F

Dear Colonel
Dr Trall, for one, is in favour of it. On a Walk, he suggests,
'you can point out the various objects of Interest –
perchance some lofty Mountain Peak, or lowly Glen,
elegant Mansions or lowly vine-clad Cottages, the gay
Equipages of the wealthy, or the noble and manly Sons
of Toil as they walk, living pictures of Health, Innocence
and Happiness to their daily avocations'.[44]

                                              Prudence

Dear Prudence
We see no need to teach our Innocent and Curly-haired
Child the so-called Facts of Life.
                                              Alderman R deLisle J.

Dear Alderman
I can do no more than Quote a pure-minded Author, who
writes: 'O, ridiculous Fathers and Mothers! – do ye not

know that the Unarmoured Ignorance of your curly-haired Darlings will certainly be exposed to the Fury of Ignorant Vice? and the foolish Ignorance of your Daughters will tend to Pamper, rather than Destroy, the Impurity of other Sons than yours?'[16]

Prudence

'. . . the Unarmoured Ignorance of your curly-haired Darlings will certainly be exposed to the Fury of Ignorant Vice'

Dear Prudence
Having read your warning to the Alderman, we should like to teach our unarmoured Child the Facts of Life, starting with Plants. Does the Lettuce, for example, have Sexual Intercourse?

A Puzzled Parent

Dear Puzzled
I am afraid it does. 'Speaking plainly, it is the Sexual Intercourse of Plant life from which baby Plants are produced. Sexual science in Human life bears such a close analogy to Plant life that it should be taught with the same Freedom and Reverence.'[39]

Prudence

Dear Prudence
We have introduced our Children to the Marriage Ceremony
of Flowers, and the birth of the baby Bud. Should they
now consider the transfer of Pollen in the Mammal and
the Human?

Materfamilias

'they can approach one
another for that Purpose,
when they are
Grown Up and Strong'

Dear Mater

You can scarcely do better than to use the words of Miss
Ethelmer, who writes as follows: 'Mammals and Humans
have no need of Bees or Moths to transfer the Pollen
substance from the Male to the Female; for they can
approach one another for that Purpose, when they are
Grown Up and Strong. Indeed, they *do* so approach at
certain times, in order that the Ovules of the Female may
receive some of the Pollen substance.'[13]

This should make everything clear.

Prudence

7
ON THE TRAINING OF YOUNG LADIES

Dear Prudence
A young lady of my Acquaintance has allowed herself to
kiss a Man, of the Opposite Sex, to whom she is not
Affianced. In these circumstances, can you offer the least
Comfort?

A Soul in Anguish

Dear Soul
I fear there is little Comfort to be offered. 'In the case of
Females, they have practically only one chance in life.
One step in a wild, mad hour of Passionate Delirium, and
for ever afterwards, the Woman hears the Clang of
Chains, and the Knell of Despair.'[48]

This Prospect need not
Unduly Disturb your Friend.
There remains a possibility
of Redemption beyond
the Grave.

Prudence

'. . . ever afterwards,
the Woman hears the
Clang of Chains,
and the Knell of Despair'

Dear Prudence
My Daughter has taken to the Reading of Novels and to
supporting her Skirts from her Hips. Will either of these
Habits reduce her to a State of Sexual Infirmity?

A Lady

Dear Lady
Probably both. 'The causes of Sexual Infirmity in Young
Women are: rich unwholesome Food, supporting the
weight of their Dresses and Skirts from the Hips, Novel-
reading, and the keeping of Late Hours.'[38]

Prudence

Dear Prudence
I take it that a Girl is unfit for Marriage before the full
maturity of Womanhood?

Country Doctor

Dear Doctor
She is Unfit for more than Marriage. One of your Medical
Colleagues has wisely written, of the Girl under twenty-
five years, that 'her Bones are soft: her Muscles are soft:
and her Brain is also'.[25]

Prudence

Dear Prudence
My Daughters have recently attended a Soirée at which
Kissing Games were played and Dancing permitted. Are
these not Steep and Gilded Paths to the Region of Fire
which Fly in the face of Nature?

A Troubled Guardian

Dear Guardian
Steep and Gilded indeed. Dr Goss writes: 'Nature will have
none of it! She has issued her Manifesto. Kissing games
must be confined to the tiniest of Children, if permissible
at all. The Dance must be eliminated. All familiarities
among people of opposite sexes must be resolutely aban-
doned and denounced.'[17]

The late Samuel Morley goes further. Would you not, he asks parents, 'ten thousand times rather your beautiful Daughter had a dagger put through her Pure heart, or a bullet through her brain, than that she be forced to submit to inhuman, diabolical Outrages, to the nature of which it is impossible even to allude'.[48]

I trust this will settle the question of Kissing Games.

        Prudence

'Would you not . . .
rather your beautiful
Daughter had a dagger
put through her Pure Heart?'

8
ON THE FUNCTION OF WOMAN

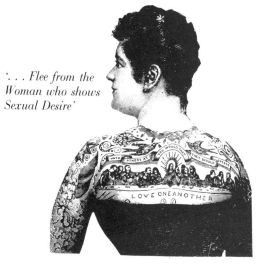

*'. . . Flee from the
Woman who shows
Sexual Desire'*

*Dear Prudence
I am married to a Woman who Demands the Conjugal
Relation. Should she not merely Respond to my Desires?*
                                    Disturbed Husband

Dear Disturbed
According to an expert on Women, 'embraces are rarely
sought by the Wife, or her Desire for them indicated.
They should occur only at the solicitation of the Husband,
when his Desires are ardent, and when her own are
not'.[41] To which Dr Stall adds that any Man should Flee
from the Woman who shows Sexual Desire. 'To make
her your Wife would be deliberately to Blight your Life,
to Blast your Happiness, and render impossible the
Happiness and Blessing that would likely and reasonably

be yours, if married to a Pure-minded Woman.'[38]

Of course, in your married state, you may not find this advice much Consolation.

Prudence

Dear Prudence
I come of a Respectable Family, and wish to marry a decent young man from the Labouring Class. May I hope, in this way, to elevate and refine him?

Adelaide Jane Priscilla W

Dear Adelaide Jane
Observe this law: 'A Man marrying a Woman beneath him may raise her to any Eminence that he himself may reach; but if a Woman marry a Man beneath her, she always goes down to his Level.'[41]

Only you can decide whether Social Ruin is your Ambition in Life.

Prudence

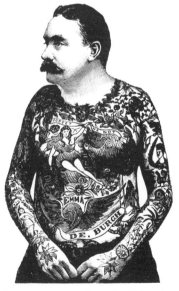

'. . . *a decent young man from the Labouring Class*'

31

Dear Prudence
Can you tell me why there are Six Per Cent more Men
than Women? I assume it is the Creator's way of providing
for the Armed Forces of our Empire?

A Devout Patriot

Dear Devout
Certainly our Soldiers are a part of the Divine Purpose. In
an ideal world, writes an eminent Doctor, 'the bountiful
provision of Nature, whereby Male children outnumber
Female children by a hundred and six to a hundred,
would be maintained up to Adult Life; the extra Six Men
affording the necessary margin for Soldiers, Sailors, Pion-
eers, Missionaries and Ascetics'.[33]

Prudence

Dear Prudence
It seems, to a Detached Observer, that Woman, in her
Grosser Manifestations, is closely akin to the Brutes of
the Natural World. Are there Authorities who support this
View?

Disgusted

Dear Disgusted
There are, indeed, Authorities who go further than you
yourself. According to Mr Terry, 'the monthly period of
woman is the same in general Character and Purpose as
the period of Heat in the Females of Brutes. It is, however,
much more intense. In the Woman, this desire often lasts
the whole month through.'[41] Manifestly, you have every
Reason to be Repelled.

Prudence

Dear Prudence
Exactly what is the Function of Woman?

Puzzled

Dear Puzzled
This is a frequent, but easily resolved, question. 'The
normal Condition of Woman is declared by the Holy Writ
to be Marriage.'[35] Enlarging upon this, Mr Parkhurst has
said that 'the greatest thing a Woman can do is to do the
thing that she was specifically Endowed and Ordained to
do, and that is to bear Children and train them for the
Uses and Service of the World they are born into'.[31]

                                                    Prudence

Dear Prudence
My Wife shows signs of wishing to venture outside the
Family Home. Am I correct in Circumscribing this
presumptuous Desire?   *A Newly Married Husband*

Dear Newly Married
Entirely correct. Her place is Within, yours Without. Or,
as it has been phrased, 'while the Home is the Mother's
world, the World is the Father's home'.[31]   Prudence

Dear Prudence
While it is generally accepted that Woman is mentally
Inferior to Man, the Reasons are unclear. What has Science
to say on the subject?   *Philosopher*

Dear Philosopher
Science has a good deal to say on the subject. According
to one scientist, 'Men are guided by their Intellects only,
while Women are guided by their Hearts only,'[10] However,
a writer in the *Westminster Review* has suggested that 'the
Mental Inferiority which we ascribe to our Women may
be wholly due to the habits of our Nation, which do not
allow to Women the same Mental Exercise as Men'.[43]
Nature or Nurture: the choice is yours.

                                                    Prudence

9

ON THE PLIGHT OF THE 'PROGRESSIVE' WOMAN

Dear Prudence
I find it hard, I must confess, to maintain a Proper Subordination to the Man who is now my Spouse.

A Progressive Woman

Dear 'Progressive'
Why should it be so terrible, asks Dr Goss, to acknowledge that your Husband is nobler and larger than yourself?
Be thankful it is so. Try to climb up on his broad Shoulders and see the world through his eyes. What an opportunity, to be in close contact with an Intelligence and Character so much greater than your own . . .
Bend your proud little neck to the Yoke of his Judgment. Be less assertive and aggressive. Sit at his feet and learn. Sometimes his Mind will have so much wider sweep than yours that it will be far better for you to be like a Child than a Wife'.[17] I have no doubt that you will find these Sentiments a Consolation.   Prudence

'. . . acknowledge that your Husband is nobler and larger than yourself'

34

'certain Women, of the "advanced" sort, wish to work outside the Home'

Dear Prudence
I have heard that certain Women, of the 'advanced' sort, wish to work outside the Home. Surely such Practice unfits the Female for her true Duty of Motherhood?
                        A Plain Labouring Man

Dear Plain
It has been well said that working women 'so sorely affect the Natural Functions of their Sex that, with the exception of a small proportion of them, they can never wholly Regain the Conditions necessary in order to discharge the Duties of Maternity in a manner which is easy to themselves or satisfactory to their Child – if, indeed, they ever Produce one'.[21]

   To which, Mr Terry adds that 'the Workers of our Race are necessarily the Men. It is these that are specially Fitted for the task. To the Woman is given the work of continuing the Race'.[41]
                        Prudence

Dear Prudence
I hear that short-haired young women now proclaim
Equality between the Sexes, and seek 'careers' for the
Weaker Sex. What do our Authorities have to say on the
subject of these Propositions?

Homo Sapiens

Dear Homo
The Authorities have a great deal to say. 'Any approach
to natural "equality" between Man and Woman,' writes
Mr Heape, 'is rendered absolutely Impossible, so far as
Nature and her Purposes are concerned.'[21]

Let us leave the final word with an eminent Writer,
who cries: 'Great Heavens! – while there are young Men
in the world, what "career" do Women want opened out
for them? What more arduous task do they desire than
to influence for Good the Male Hearts that are in their
Power?'[16]

What indeed?

Prudence

Dear Prudence
How shall we Address those Young Women who would
Cohabit in some Rotten Relationship which lacks the
Benefit of Marriage?

The End of Civilization

Dear End of Civilization
We can do no better than echo the Doctor who writes that
'those living together Without Marriage would be Slaves
to their own Passions and Lusts'.[33]

Let us cry also, in the words of Dr Goss, that 'only as
Heroic and Indomitable an Effort as was made to save
Holland from Spain can preserve human society from
Polygamy, Polyandry, Free Love, or some other Age-Old
and Rotten form of Relationship between the Sexes'.[17]

Prudence

Dear Prudence
I assume we may Confidently Assert, then, that Marriage
is the pinnacle of Nature's Progression? There will be no
more advanced Arrangement for Blessing the Union of the
Sexes?
                                    Follower of the Light

Dear Follower
Certainly there will not. 'Marriage is the final Act of
Nature's selection among all other Possible
Relationships.'¹⁷
                                    Prudence

Dear Prudence
I am unwilling to seem Doubtful; but how can we be
Certain that Nature has nothing Else planned?
                          Troubled Follower of the Light

Dear Troubled Follower
Nature, says Dr Goss, 'proclaims upon the Housetop, and
with a Note of Unwavering Assurance: "This is the True
Relationship between Male and Female members of the
Race. I have tried them all. The Rest are False!"'¹⁷

   I trust this, Troubled, sets your Mind at Ease.
                                    Prudence

'some other Age-Old and Rotten form of Relationship between the
Sexes'

37

Dear Prudence
What are we to say of those Strong-Minded Women who
now call themselves Feminists?
                                    One who is not Afraid to
                                    Call Herself a Wife and Mother

Dear One who is not Afraid
Let us simply say that 'a "strong-minded" Woman is a
satire on her Sex. She becomes Officious, Forward,
Meddlesome and a "Busybody in other *Men's* matters",
which is far worse than if it were other *Women's* matters'.[22]
And let us recall the wise dictum that 'it is futile for
Woman to deplore the Existence of those Natural Laws
which impel her to act as a Woman, which prevent her
from acting like a Man . . . even if she would. Woman
cannot escape from the Consequences of her Natural
Functions.'[21]
                                                        Prudence

Dear Prudence
I have heard certain shameless young Ladies speak of Trial
Marriage. Surely no Modest Christian could Countenance
the Notion?
                                              Marital Bliss

Dear Bliss
No: indeed she could not. There are, according to Mr
Mantegazza, 'savages who, before giving themselves
forever, make a Trial on both sides, and separate or Marry,
according to the result of the experience. But such Moral
and Modest People as we are, must content ourselves with
Guessing'.[26]
                                                        Prudence

Dear Prudence
Should we not Pity those who remain Outside the State of
Matrimony?
                                      Milk of Human Kindness

Dear Milk
On the contrary: unmarried persons are, as Mr Heape says, 'living abnormal lives. Nature has designed that they should be Fathers and Mothers, and if they do not fulfil the Laws of Nature, they must suffer'.[21]

Prudence

Dear Prudence
What would you say to One who has Chosen to Remain a Bachelor?

Unwed at Fifty

Dear Unwed
I should say, in the words of a noted Writer, 'that all Crimes laid together cannot Equal yours. You are guilty of Murder in not Suffering those to be Born which should proceed from you'.[23]

Let me know if you have any other questions.

Prudence

Dear Prudence
For the last seven years I have been Courting a Young Lady who refuses to Marry. How can one Interpret such Behaviour?

Unconsummated Suitor

Dear Unconsummated
It may be that she does not like you. On the other hand, it has been asserted that 'ladies of this Class cherish a kind of Malicious and Insane Pleasure in causing Pain; and when with Love the Soul is widely opened to its lowest Depths, they fill it full of Wormwood. The stinging Satire of such meek-eyed Vixens is abominable'.[22]

You might well consider, within the next few years, drawing your Courtship to a close.

Prudence

10

On Evil Practices

Dear Prudence
My Chums at school have recently introduced me to the
Solitary Vice. Will this Evil pass in the Coming Decades?
An Erring Lad

Dear Erring
I do not wish to depress you, at a tender age, but you are
unlikely ever to be free of the Vice. I had a letter recently,
from a Gentleman, over fifty years of age, who has been
struggling against the Evil Habits of Boyhood for *nearly*

'My Chums at school have recently introduced me to the
Solitary Vice'

forty years: and whose life to him is now a Burden and a Curse. If he had been Warned in his Youth, what might he not have been?'[20]

By the same token, what might *you* not have been, had you written earlier?

Prudence

'. . . a Gentleman who has been struggling against the Evil Habits of Boyhood for nearly forty years'

Dear Prudence
Some Boys, of evil reputation, have told me that the Sexual Member can be developed through Exercise. Is this True? Or, as I suppose, no more than a temptation to Solitary Vice?

Underdeveloped

Dear Underdeveloped
'This false and ruinous idea,' says Dr Stall, 'comes from the fact that the Muscles are strengthened by Exercise. But, instead of being Developed by this Unnatural Process, the Sexual Member is itself impaired; and if the process is often Repeated, or Long Continued, the result is the Dwarfing and Wasting of the Organ itself and the complete shattering of the entire Nervous System.'[38]

It seems, Underdeveloped, that you can expect little Beneficent Change.

Prudence

41

Dear Prudence
Do the Crocodile or the Hedgehog, I wonder, practise the Solitary Vice?
An Observer of Nature

Dear Observer
There are, apparently, 'occasional instances of this kind'.[38] Fortunately, 'they are entirely exceptional, and are accomplished with the Utmost Difficulty'; as you may well imagine.
Prudence

For the Crocodile, the Solitary Vice is entirely exceptional and accomplished with the Utmost Difficulty

Dear Prudence
Do other Crocodiles, or Hedgehogs, learn from this Vile Behaviour?
A Second Naturalist

Dear Naturalist
No they do not. 'Even where other Animals have Witnessed the Act, they do not attempt it by Imitation.'[38]
I hope this satisfies what I can only regard as an Unnatural Curiosity.
Prudence

Dear Prudence
My Girl Friend is both Sensual and Smelly as to the Feet. Does this indicate the Secret Vice of Self Abuse?
A Moral Young Lady

Dear Moral
Your Friend may simply need to wash. On the other hand, such Feet do suggest the Solitary Vice. The Symptoms are these: 'the Face loses its colour and the Eye grows

dull, heavy and weak; the Hands feel soft and clammy, and often the smell of the Feet is Unbearable . . . These are only the Heralds of more terrible things to come, such as Epilepsy, Insanity, and a mighty Host of Innumerable Evils, all of them paving the Way, too sadly, and too surely, to a Premature Grave'.[48]

All in all, your Friend might be well advised to seek some other Diversion.

Prudence

Dear Prudence
At what Tender Age should we start to Watch for the evils of Solitary Vice?

Sleepless Nights

Dear Sleepless
If you wish to prevent Rickets and Fits, you can scarcely start your watch too soon. 'I call to mind the sad case of a little Girl, *between two and three years old*, who was in the Habit of amusing herself by playing with her Private Parts, thus not only encouraging the Sinful Habit at that early age, but predisposing herself to Rickets, Spinal Weakness, Stammering, Fits, etcetera.'[48] One shudders to think what that 'etcetera' may comprehend.

Prudence

Dear Prudence
I have heard that the Solitary Vice is possible through Thought, even without Mechanical Intervention. *I find this Difficult to Credit.*

Sceptic

Dear Sceptic
Would that it were not so. But Mrs Wood-Allen writes that 'Girls who would not stoop to a Mechanical Exciting of themselves do so through Thoughts; and do not know that they are just as Guilty of Self Abuse as the Girl who uses the Hand or other Mechanical Means'.[47]

Prudence

Dear Prudence
On my journey home from work,
I am Accosted, and Tempted, by
Loose Women. How should I deal
with this Snare and Delusion?
           Scylla and Charybdis

Dear Scylla
When approached by a Prostitute,
writes Mr Dyer, 'instead of
Sinning, think of her Mother,
young man, whose Heart in
some distant home, perhaps,
is breaking because of
her Child's fall . . .
Speak to her of
Home and God,
and give her at
least a sum
large enough
to start her
back to her
Mother's arms.'[12]
   It is only fair to Warn that
paying for the Lady's journey
back to her Mother's arms
should be done with Discretion.
The purpose of your donation
may not be immediately
obvious to the onlooker.
                    Prudence

'I am Accosted, and Tempted,
by Loose Women'

Dear Prudence
I have Succumbed to Temptation and Caressed a Young
Lady; by whom I was not Shunned. Am I right in
Supposing that there can be no Expiation for such a
grievous Lapse?

Repentant Sinner

'Succumbed to Temptation
and Caressed a
Young Lady'

Dear Repentant
Yours, writes Mr Green, 'is a double guilt. Your guilt is
not of your Sin alone, for you have a part of her
Damnation whom you lead to Sin. Upon her head, though
stained with constant Guilt, your hand lays a fresh
Burden; your sin adds to her Condemnation; your Hand
is stained with a Scarlet, and all the Waters of the Earth
can never cleanse that Hand.'[19]

It seems that you are right in your Supposition.

Prudence

Dear Prudence
My Fiancé wishes to experiment with the Marital Embrace,
though we are not yet Wed. Should I Succumb to his
Wild Entreaties? Or not?
Primrose Path

Dear Primrose
Much depends how you wish to spend your future years.
It is recorded that, not many weeks since, 'a respectable
Young Woman was engaged to a Man. In an unguarded
moment she Fell: when she woke up to the Realization
of her True Position, her Mind was filled with Despair.
Eventually, she went raving Mad. Since then, she has
been the Inmate of an Asylum'.[48]

 If I were you, I should weigh the Decision with some
Care.
               Prudence

11
ON IMMORALITY

Dear Prudence
I write with a Delicate and Painful problem. In public
places (such as the Omnibus) I am Embarrassed by the
Unsolicited Erection of my Member. Can you suggest a
Cause or Cure?
                                    Unwillingly Upright

Dear Upright
Leaving aside Old Age, there is no Cure; but the Cause
may well be your own Immorality. According to Dr Stall,
'a Troublesome Result of Sexual Transgression is a quite
Continuous and Painful Erection of the Sexual
Member'.[38]
   You could, of course, cease to use the Omnibus.
                                    Prudence

Dear Prudence
I am engaged to a Young Man whose Movements are
Curious. Might this suggest Immorality? Or, perhaps, the
Suppression of Sexual Excitement?
                                    Perplexed and Betrothed

Dear Perplexed
It is hard to tell, since you fail to mention whether your
fiancé is also an Imbecile.
   According to Dr Blackwell, 'sexual Sensations, when
Inordinately Excited, will at once call into play Respon-
dent Movements. A state of a very similar kind exists in
many Idiots, in whom the Sexual Propensity exerts a
Dominant Power.'[3]
                                    Prudence

Dear Prudence
My Husband is Inclined to use his Mouth, in Unusual
Fashion, during the Marital Embrace. Can you Suggest
the likely Result of such Perversion?
And should he not Stop it
forthwith?

      A Stricken Wife

'that Grave is always
under his Feet, go
where he may'

Dear Stricken
Just such a Deviant has been graphically described as
'sitting by the Wayside of Life. Poor man, he is attending
his own Funeral: he made his own Coffin: yes, drove every
Nail: sole Chaplain of his own funeral Rites, and sole
Mourner of his own Bereavement, he reads that awful
Burial Service for souls Lost and Dead in Life: his great
wild Heart is put into a Grave that is wet with nothing
save his own Tears: and oh! Horrid Thought! that Grave
is always under his Feet, go where he may; and the Hollow
Murmur of the Present Tomb is always singing, like the
Plaintive Moan of the Ocean Shell, a Lost Life's requiem
in the Wanderer's ear.'[22]

    With regard to your second question: yes, he probably
should stop.

                        Prudence

12

ON MATTERS PERTAINING TO THE BODY

Dear Prudence
How can I improve my Hands, which are Stained in a
most Unfeminine Fashion?
                                        Daughter of Toil

Dear Daughter
It is recorded that 'Country Girls frequently hold their
Hands to a whirling Grindstone, which speedily Removes
all Stains and Blemishes'.[32]

Lacking a Grindstone, you might try the Depilatory
described below. Given time, it will remove almost
anything.

                                        Prudence

Dear Prudence
Although I know that Marriage is the Highest Achievement
of the Female, I am Unnaturally Hairy; and therefore
unwilling to Wed.
                                        Henrietta

Dear Henrietta
What you need is a Depilatory, which you can make in
the following way. 'Quick lime, one ounce; alkaline Lye,
one-half pint; orpiment and red Arsenic, one-half ounce.
Boil and try till the right strength is obtained, then touch
the Hair carefully.'[32]

Should you not have the Mixture correct, your skin will
doubtless grow again. But you will Appreciate that the
Result may do nothing to hasten the Marriage you seek.
                                        Prudence

Dear Prudence
My Husband spends much of the Night sitting in the Bath
or standing in the Shower. Is this Unusual?

Wondering Wife

Dear Wondering
Uncomfortable, rather than Unusual. 'Plentiful Sponging
of the Body,' says the Reverend Ashington Bullen, 'and
sitting in Cold Water, are invaluable means of repressing
Unchaste Desires.'[+]

I presume that your Husband has such Desires: at least
in the early Hours of the Evening?

If not, you are right to be puzzled.

Prudence

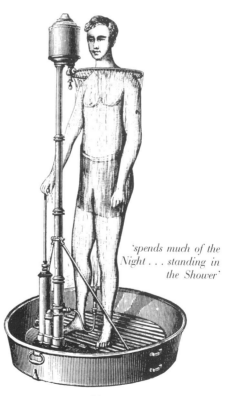

*'spends much of the
Night . . . standing in
the Shower'*

13

ON LEISURE

Dear Prudence
Our Neighbours suggest we accompany them to the
Theatre. Should we go?
                                                Cautious Couple

Dear Cautious
First, find out how your Neighbours pass the Sabbath. 'A
great many Fathers and Mothers repair to the Theatre in
the evening, leaving the House and Family in charge of
an Irish Nurse until the small hours of the Morning, and
then go to bed with Heated Imaginations and, if the next
day be the Sabbath, they lie in all day to Cool Off for
Monday morning.'[2]
    Consider whether a trip to the Theatre justifies spending
your Weekend in this way.
                                                Prudence

Dear Prudence
I have been invited to a Dance, and wonder whether this
will lead me to Sin?

Virgo Intacta

Dear Intacta

Much depends on your religion. 'A Bishop of the Roman
Catholic Church has stated that the work of the
Confessional revealed that Nineteen out of every Twenty
who fell into Sin, confess the beginning of their Sad State
to the Modern Dance.'[38]

However, you will not find the same Proportion of
Sinners (or, indeed, of Dancers) in the Methodist Church.

Prudence

'Nineteen out of every Twenty . . .
confess the beginning of their
Sad State to the
Modern Dance'

14

ON THE HORRIBLE EFFECTS
OF ALCOHOL

Dear Prudence
A man of my Acquaintance has drunk Wine daily for
many years, without the Evil Consequences which I
confidently expected.   *Disappointed Teetotaller*

Dear Disappointed
Ah, but what of his Offspring? Mrs Wood-Allen writes of
a man 'who boasted that he had used a Bottle of Wine
daily for Fifty Years, and it had not injured him: but of
his Twelve Children, *six died in Infancy, one was Imbe-*
cile, one was Insane, and the rest were Hysterical
Invalids'.[47]
  I trust this Intelligence tempers your Disappointment.
                                        Prudence

Dear Prudence
I suspect that my Husband has Taken to Drink. How
should I Confirm or Deny this Secret Suspicion?

Sleepless Nights

Dear Sleepless
Dr Stall recommends the following Test. 'Take from the
Arm of the Inveterate Drinker a small Quantity of Blood,
apply a Match, and the Presence of Alcohol is immediately
indicated by a Lurid Flame.'[38]   This Procedure may,
of course, arouse your Husband's curiosity. You would do
well to have your story prepared in advance.

Prudence

'I suspect that my Husband has Taken to Drink'

Dear Prudence
My Husband, normally an Abstemious Man, drank several
Toasts on the Day of our Wedding. Will this Disadvan-
tage our Unborn Infants?

Mother-To-Be

Dear Mother-To-Be
I must ask, in turn, whether you regard Idiocy as a
disadvantage? Dr Trall writes of 'cases in which, from
the Feastings and Drinkings which Celebrated the Wedding
Occasion, the first-born were rendered Idiots'.[43]

   Short of Celibacy, however, there is not much you can
do about it now.

Prudence

15
ON DRESS AND DEPORTMENT

'. . . this is the Secret History of half the Cases that come into the Divorce Courts'

Dear Prudence
Should I wear Stays?

No Longer a Nymph

Dear Nymph
Through wearing stays, 'the Woman becomes a lymphatic Log; the Husband disgusted; and there cannot be the faintest Doubt whatever, that this is the Secret History of half the Cases that come into the Divorce Courts'.[16]

However, you must make your own choice. Prudence

Dear Prudence
Now that I am a Young Lady, it has
been suggested I should adopt the
Custom of wearing Knickers, or
Drawers. Can you tell me
whether I should do so; and
Why such Garments are
Worn? Do they, perhaps,
protect the Private Parts
from Dust?
Ungirt Loins

Dear Ungirt Loins
You are perfectly correct
in your assumption.
'Ladies and Gentlemen
wear Drawers now, at
all seasons. Gentlemen
require them in order
to protect the Outer
Clothing from
Perspiration; while
Ladies wear them for
Protection from Dust,
and to avoid accidental
exposures.'24

Prudence

'to avoid accidental exposures'

16

ON FOREIGN LANDS AND CUSTOMS

Dear Prudence
I am considering Marriage to an American. Is it possible
for such a Union to be Blessed with Issue?
                                        An English Maid

Dear English Maid
Possible, but not necessarily desirable. According to Mr
Mantegazza, 'the crossing of a Superior Race with an
Inferior One lowers the First and elevates the Second'.[26]
    I fear that this Consideration may Explain your Fiancé's
proposal.
                                        Prudence

Dear Prudence
My husband, a Churchman, has – against my Expressed
Wish – invited a visiting Negro preacher to dine with us.
Can you instruct me as to what such a Person is likely to
Eat?
                                        Reluctant Hostess

Dear Reluctant
I can do no better than refer you to Mr Carroll, who states
that, 'although the Negro is omnivorous, he Manifests a
Strong Preference for the Flesh of Man as an article of
Food'.[6]
    My best wishes for the dinner party.
                                        Prudence

Dear Prudence
When seated in Polite Society, should the Feet be Above or Below the Head?

Puzzled

'the Custom of sitting with the Feet elevated above the Head'

Dear Puzzled
This is a common problem, but one which can be easily resolved. 'The Custom of sitting with the Feet elevated above the Head is believed to be purely American in origin, and generally confined to that Continent in its Practice. It can scarcely be considered either Useful or Ornamental.'[24]

Prudence

Dear Prudence
For some time, numerous Acquaintances have insisted on using my Pocket Handkerchief. Can you tell me whether this is Acceptable in more Refined Circles?

Priscilla

Dear Priscilla
You would do well to curtail your generosity. 'To use the same Towel or Pocket Handkerchief requires the closest Personal Intimacy, and this should never be Presumed on.'[24]

Prudence

Dear Prudence
Are Australians more Stupid than other Humans; or is
this an Unconfirmed Prejudice?
                                    Anti-Antipodean

Dear Anti
It is certainly not unconfirmed. According to Mr William
Parker, 'the average weight of the Australian Brain is 907
grammes. The Significance of this appears when we learn
that . . . if the Brain falls below 978 grammes, the result
is Idiocy.'[6]
    After all, why else would they live in Australia?
                                    Prudence

Dear Prudence
We are considering a Sojourn in France. I suppose that we
must Expect a sad Falling Off in Standards of Conjugal
Fidelity?
                                    Albion

Dear Albion
You must indeed. According
to Major Seton Churchill,
'married Englishmen do lead
Pure Lives: the married
Frenchman is proverbially
Untrue to his Wife'.[10]
                Prudence

'. . . the Frenchman is
proverbially Untrue
to his Wife'

Dear Prudence
Is there Hope for the Savage who remains untouched by
the Blessings of Empire? You will understand that I refer,
in particular, to the Negro.
                                                    Outer Darkness

Dear Darkness
According to the eminent Black Writer,
Mr Alfred Ernest Tracey, the history
of Nations is full of reassurance for
the Negro. 'Many a Savage Son of
Ethiopia now Grovelling in the
Impenetrable Darkness of
Fetishism and Uncivilization,
may ultimately be brought
within the Radii of the
Ever-Glorious Light of the World,
to be Rewarded with the White
Robe of Innocence, Purity and
Truth.'[42]

   However, Mr Tracey urges us
to recall that the Negro 'is at
least a Thousand Years behind
his Caucasian brother in the
Race for Perfection; and has
only within the last Half-Century
been brought within the Beneficent
Influence of Ethical Science'.
   So be not Impatient, Outer
Darkness. In the task of Reforming
our Dusky Relation, what
Matters an odd Millennium?
                         Prudence

'Many a Savage Son of Ethiopia . . . may ultimately be brought
within the Radii of the Ever-Glorious Light of the World'

60

17

ON THE TWILIGHT YEARS

Dear Prudence
While I am only now reaching the Prime of Life, my
Spouse, in her forties, has become scarcely Female.
                                    King David

Dear David
Unfortunately, this is an inescapable part of Nature's plan.
'A Man may be a Man at Eighty Years of Age . . . a
Woman, on the Contrary, after Forty-Five, is no longer a
Woman.'[26]
                                    Prudence

'. . . a Woman, after Forty-Five, is no longer a Woman'

'Excesses committed at a time when their Enfeebled Powers are unable to Support them'

Dear Prudence
My Wife, at the age of Forty, combines unflagging
Enthusiasm for the Marital Embrace with Declining Intel-
ligence. Are the two Phenomena connected?
                                           Autumn of Life

Dear Autumn
Almost certainly they are. Dr Napheys writes that 'many
Affections of the Brain, under which Elderly Persons
suffer, and to which a certain Proportion annually
Succumbs, are caused by Excesses committed at a time
when their Enfeebled Powers are unable to Support
them'.[37]

Either One, or Both of you, would be well advised to
spend your Nights in a Cold Bath.
                                           Prudence

Dear Prudence
I have Recently been a little Bereaved. Should I therefore
wear Black?
                                    Intimations of Mortality

Dear Intimations
Not necessarily. According to a Member of the Aristocracy,
'we do not Advise people to Rush into Black for every
Slight Bereavement'.[28]

On the other hand, even a Passing Brush with the
Reaper will make Festive Apparel inappropriate.

                                    Prudence

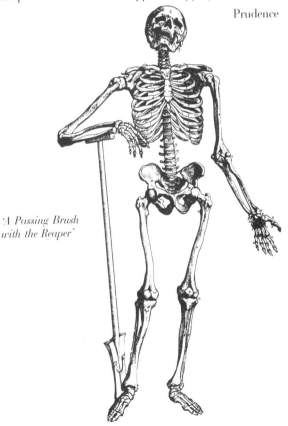

*'A Passing Brush
with the Reaper'*

Gerard Macdonald is a New Zealander who now lives in Sussex with his wife and (when they are at home) two children. He writes mainly for television and film, apart from occasional excursions into children's fiction and Victorian advice.